So You Want To Work In

Travel and Tourism?

Margaret McAlpine

WAYLAND

© Copyright Wayland 2004

Editor: Patience Coster
Inside design: Peta Morey
Cover design: Wayland

Published in Great Britain in 2004 by Hodder Wayland,
an imprint of Hodder Children's Books.

This paperback edition published in 2008 by Wayland

All rights reserved. Apart from any use permitted under UK copyright law, this publication may only be reproduced, stored or transmitted, in any form, or by any means with prior permission in writing of the publishers or in the case of reprographic production in accordance with the terms of licences issued by the Copyright Licensing Agency.

British Library Cataloguing Publication Data
McAlpine, Margaret
So you want to work in travel & tourism?
1.Tourism – Vocational guidance – Juvenile literature
I.Title
388.4'7910'23

ISBN 9780750254809

Picture Acknowledgements. The publishers would like to thank the following for allowing their pictures to be reproduced in this publication: Daniel Samuel Robbins / Corbis 4, 39; Larry Williams / Corbis 5, 32, 37, 59 (top); Earl Kowall / Corbis 6; Neil Rabinowitz / Corbis 7, 11 (top); Dave Bartruff / Corbis 8; Paul A. Souders / Corbis 9; Kevin Schafer / Corbis 11(bottom); Firefly Productions / Corbis 12; Bernard Annebicque / Corbis 13; Patrik Giardino / Corbis 14; Lew Long / Corbis 15; Getty Images 16, 19 (bottom); Najiah Feanny-Hicks / Corbis 17; Corbis all borders, 19 (top), 31. 53; Richard E.Cummins / Corbis 20; Richard T. Nowitz / Corbis 21; Bob Rowan / Corbis 22, 25, 27 (top); Eric K. K. Yu / Corbis 23; Barbara Peacock / Corbis 24; Frederic Neema / Corbis 27 (bottom); Daniel Mirer / Corbis 28; David Ball / Corbis 29; Alan Schein / Corbis 30; Kelly / Mooney / Corbis 33; Dann Tardif / Corbis 35 (top); Ariel Skelley / Corbis 35 (bottom), 43 (top); Jon Feingersh / Corbis 36; Edward Holub / Corbis 38; Connie Ricca / Corbis 40; Roger Ressmeyer / Corbis 41; Richard Bickel / Corbis 43; George Shelley / Corbis 44, 51; Jose Luis Pelaez, Inc / Corbis 45; Gabe Palmer / Corbis 46, 47; Tony Demin / Corbis 48; Michael Keller / Corbis 49; Claudia Kunin / Corbis 50; Darama / Corbis 52; Carl Purcell / Corbis 54; Richard T. Nowitz / Corbis 55; Sally Wiener Grotta / Corbis 56; Tom Stewart / Corbis 57; Steve Prezant / Corbis 59 (bottom).

Printed in China

Wayland
338 Euston Road
London NW1 3BH

Wayland is an imprint of Hachette Children's Books, an Hachette Livre UK Company.

Note: Photographs illustrating the 'day in the life of' pages are posed by models.

Kingston Upon Hull City Council	
Askews	
J338	£8.99

Contents

Cruise Liner Officer	4
Flight Attendant	12
Hotel Manager	20
Theme Park Attractions Manager	28
Tour Guide	36
Travel Agent	44
Travel Writer	52
Glossary	60
Further Information	62
Index	64

Words in **bold** can be found in the glossary.

Cruise Liner Officer

What is a cruise liner officer?

Cruise liner officers work on ships which carry people rather than **cargo**. The passengers on board a cruise liner have the opportunity to enjoy a great social life, wonderful food and entertainment. At the same time they visit different places of interest around the world and spend days sightseeing on dry land.

Cruise liners usually sail around a particular area, such as the Caribbean or the Mediterranean, stopping off at different ports during the day and sailing through the night. While passengers enjoy themselves, the staff on board work hard to make sure that everything runs smoothly. The captain is in overall charge of the ship, its passengers and crew. On board, the captain's word is final.

Life at sea is hard work for the crew and great fun for the passengers.

Floating hotels

An increasing number of people are taking holidays several times a year and cruises are becoming very popular. Many modern cruise ships are like floating holiday resorts with **casinos**, theatres, cinemas, beauty salons, fitness centres, shops and even golf courses. There are hundreds of staff on board to make sure that passengers have a good time, are safe and arrive on time at each port.

Cruise liner officers supervise the deck and engine operations on board ship. As the ship sails from port to port, it is the responsibility of the deck crew to ensure that the **navigating** and steering are accurate so that it keeps to its planned route. The engine room crew ensure that the machinery and equipment are well-maintained and function properly.

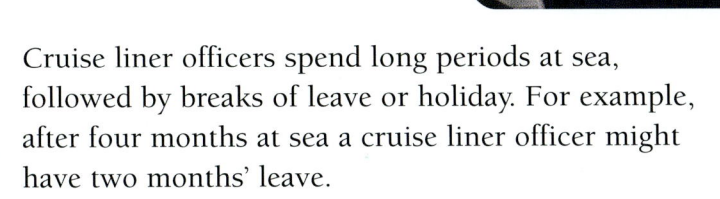

Cruise liner officers spend long periods at sea, followed by breaks of leave or holiday. For example, after four months at sea a cruise liner officer might have two months' leave.

As the passengers relax, the ship sails to the next port.

Cruise Liner Officer 5

Main tasks of a cruise liner officer

The cruise liner officers in charge of deck and engine operations have very different jobs to do.

Deck officers (or navigation officers):
- steer and **navigate** the ship using the latest satellite and **radar** navigation technology;
- check the ship's speed and the amount of fuel it uses;
- consult weather reports and study navigation routes;
- keep in touch with ships' offices and port by satellite communication;
- supervise crew members;
- look after any administrative, commercial or **legal** matters that come up while at sea;
- socialize with passengers by attending receptions and by sitting with them at dinner and make sure they are enjoying themselves.

Officers often meet and talk to the passengers over meals.

Good points and bad points

'There's nothing quite like watching the sun rise or set from the **bridge** of a ship.'

'We are encouraged to socialize with passengers and attend functions. It's part of the job, but if I'm honest, it can be quite boring after a time. I find myself answering the same questions over and over again about what life is like on board ship.'

On a cruise liner there can be up to seven deck officers, with two on duty at the same time.

Engineering officers:
- run and maintain the ship's engines, pumps and fuel systems;
- ensure that all the equipment is in good working order and carry out any necessary repairs;
- make sure that lifts, cranes, refrigeration, ventilation, and sewage treatment systems and purifiers are regularly **overhauled** and repaired.

Careful maintenance is important for health and safety on board ship. There can be up to seven engineering officers, with two on duty at the same time.

Cruise liner officers work unsocial hours on a **watch** or shift system. This usually means working four hours on and eight hours off over a 24-hour period.

Once a ship is at sea, all repair and maintenance work is the responsibility of the crew.

Cruise Liner Officer 7

Skills needed to be a cruise liner officer

Technical knowledge
Deck and engine room jobs involve the use and maintenance of modern electrical and mechanical systems. Officers undergo intensive training to make sure they can deal with any problems that arise. This is because at sea they cannot call on outside help to put things right.

Teamwork
Officers work closely with other crew members. A ship's crew is likely to be made up of people from many different countries. It is important to get on well with everyone and enjoy working as part of a group. This skill is vital on board a ship, where people live and work together for long periods.

Teamwork is important on board ship.

Communication skills
Cruise liner officers need to have good writing and speaking skills in order to keep records, write reports and give verbal instructions clearly.

Self-reliance
Cruise liner officers are away from home for months at a time. While at sea they have only limited contact with friends and family by phone, letters collected at ports, and email. They must be able to cope with occasional feelings of loneliness and homesickness.

Training takes place on land and at sea.

Leadership skills
Officers have to manage members of the crew and win their respect.

Social skills
Officers are required to meet passengers, welcome them on board, chat to them and make sure they enjoy themselves. This is an important part of a cruise liner officer's job, and he or she is expected to attend parties and dinners, even when an early night in bed with a good book seems more appealing!

fact file

Most cruise liner officers join as **cadets** and are **sponsored** by a shipping company or training organization. They study at college for qualifications, which are recognized across the world. They also gain experience working on training placements at sea.

Cruise Liner Officer

A day in the life of a cruise liner officer

Jim Bolton

Jim is 27 years old and a deck officer on a cruise liner, which is currently sailing in the Caribbean.

Midnight	I'm up and on watch. I work two four-hour watches every day. I'm still finding it difficult to believe I'm back at sea. While we have quite long periods of leave, when they are coming to an end we have to be ready to join the ship at very short notice and that is what I've just done. As a navigational officer, I'm in charge of making sure we are steering the right course.
4.00 am	I get some rest. Life on board ship is unlike any other job because of the watches we work. Luckily, working strange hours doesn't worry me and I can sleep almost anywhere. I have my own cabin with a bathroom, so life on board is quite comfortable.
12.00 pm	I'm back on **navigation** duties.
4.00 pm	I relax and have a rest, read a book and enjoy a chat with some of the other officers.
7.30 pm	It's time to smarten up and have dinner with the passengers. They all want to know what life is like on board ship. We organize guided tours so that they can see how the ship is run. They are not allowed to wander alone in areas such as the engine room for safety reasons.

Today's ships are operated using the most up-to-date technology.

Waking up in a different location every day can be exciting – but tiring!

Cruise Liner Officer 11

Flight Attendant

What is a flight attendant?

Flight attendants work in the passenger cabin of a plane and are responsible for the safety and comfort of the people on board. They serve food and drinks and deal with any problems that might arise, for example, if people become unwell. They also make sure that passengers behave properly and do not cause difficulties for other customers or for the flight crew.

Every year, millions of people travel by plane. While some planes carry around twenty passengers and travel quite short distances, others are enormous, seating up to 450 people and travelling halfway around the world.

Millions of people travel by plane every year.

Flights are either scheduled or chartered. Scheduled flights carry independent travellers, business people and tourists, all of whom are on the plane for different reasons. Charter flights carry passengers on **package tours**. These people are all going on holiday to the same area. The cost of their flight and accommodation is included in the overall price of their holiday.

12 So you want to work in travel and tourism?

The first passenger plane

In 1914 the world's first commercial passenger air service started in Florida in the USA, flying between Tampa and St Petersburg. The flight, on an **airboat**, lasted twenty minutes and there were two return journeys each day. The airboat carried a pilot and one passenger and was made out of wood, fabric and wire. After four months the service was stopped.

When they start out at their job, flight attendants usually work on short-haul flights, which last less than five hours. After gaining experience on shorter flights, they move on to long-haul flights, sometimes up to 12 hours long.

Flight attendants greet passengers and help them find their seats.

Flight Attendant

Main tasks of a flight attendant

The work of flight attendants is divided into two areas of responsibility – airline safety and customer service.

To ensure the plane is safe, flight attendants:
- check the emergency equipment and clean and tidy everything before the passengers board;
- demonstrate the use of emergency equipment, such as oxygen masks, and make sure that passengers know where the emergency exits are;
- check that passengers have their seat belts fastened before taking off and landing;
- make sure that overhead lockers are closed and gangways are clear before take-off;
- check that the captain's instructions to passengers, such as requesting that they stay seated with seat belts fastened during bad weather, are carried out.

It is important that passengers know what to do on a flight in an emergency.

Good points and bad points

'There are real perks to the job, such as cheaper flights and stopovers in great locations. Most passengers are polite and helpful.'

'Occasionally there are nightmare people, determined to make a fuss. They are noisy and rude. They don't like the food, the [in-flight] film, or the seat they've been given. Throughout the flight I have to be polite and try to calm them down.'

So you want to work in travel and tourism?

Flight attendants' responsibility for customer service includes:
- giving out meals, collecting food trays afterwards and selling drinks and snacks;
- selling **duty-free goods** such as perfume, tobacco and alcohol on international flights;
- looking after travellers with disabilities, for example wheelchair users or people with an injury such as a broken leg;
- giving first aid to anyone who falls ill during a flight;
- looking after children flying on their own without adults during the flight, and delivering them safely to another member of staff, a relative or carer on landing.

After each flight, attendants write a report about any difficulties they have encountered, such as awkward passengers, problems with meals (for example, running out of food before everyone was served) and emergency landings (because of illness, mechanical problems or bad weather).

Young children travelling alone are looked after by flight attendants.

Flight Attendant 15

Skills needed to be a flight attendant

Teamwork
Flight attendants work in small, enclosed spaces with other crew members. They need to be patient and tolerant of others, as long-haul flights can last for many hours. To look after passengers properly, flight attendants must be able to work as part of a team with other attendants and with the flight crew.

Presence of mind
Flight attendants must be able to cope when problems arise, such as sudden illness, arguments or children who are upset. They need to remain calm, think quickly and deal with the situation in a practical, sensible way.

Physical fitness
Flying can be exhausting for passengers, and a great deal worse for attendants who are working as well as travelling. Flight attendants must be fit and strong enough to cope with disturbed sleep, swollen legs (as a result of the altitude and cabin pressure), and the jet lag caused by travelling from one **time zone** to another.

First aid
When people become ill on a plane it is quite likely that medical help will not reach them for several hours. It is vital that flight attendants have first aid skills so that they can treat the patient until help arrives. The quality of their care can make a big difference to a patient's recovery.

Dealing with passengers' problems, whatever they may be, is all part of the job.

Meals and drinks help the journey pass quickly.

Customer service skills

Flight attendants ensure that passengers are relaxed and comfortable during a flight. They need to respond quickly to passengers' requests and make sure meals and drinks are served promptly. Even when the job is difficult, and people's behaviour is challenging, they have to smile and be polite and cheerful. This customer service element is central to the flight attendant's job.

fact file

Airlines are looking for the right type of person, rather than particular qualifications. They recruit flight attendants from many different backgrounds. Having said that, flight attendants must be physically fit and able to swim. Some airlines insist that flight attendants have good eyesight without the use of spectacles or contact lenses, while others accept staff wearing contact lenses.

Flight Attendant

A day in the life of a flight attendant

Peter Mendoza

Peter Mendoza is a flight attendant with a large international airline.

8.00 am	I check in for a flight from London to Tokyo and meet the crew for a pre-flight briefing. Here we exchange information about weather conditions, number of passengers and possible delays. I am one of a number of attendants on the flight. Each of us is told about our particular duties during the flight, such as dealing with special meal requests.
8.45 am	We prepare the cabin for the passengers by carrying out a safety check and making sure equipment is in place. We check that there are no unexplained or suspicious parcels on board.
9.15 am	The passengers come on board. We greet them and give them a demonstration of the safety equipment on the plane.
9.30 am	All seat belts are fastened and the plane takes off.
10.30 am	I offer the passengers tea, coffee and cold drinks.
11.30 am	Lunchtime – for the passengers at least!
1.30 pm	By this time in the flight, everyone has finished eating and we have cleared away.
2.00 pm	I take round the **duty-free goods** on a tray and afterwards make a note of what I've sold.
4.30 pm	Drinks and snack time again.

So you want to work in travel and tourism?

7.30 pm - 9.30 pm Now it's my turn to take a break and a nap.

10.00 pm We're nearly at our destination so we prepare the passengers for landing. When the plane has touched down we make sure the passengers have all their hand luggage with them. We say goodbye to them as they leave the plane.

11.30 pm We collect together our own belongings and go through the airport's **customs and immigration procedures**.

12.00 am We take a taxi to our hotel, where we look forward to a night in a comfortable bed!

Passengers can be so eager to leave the plane that they forget their hand luggage.

Another flight over, and the chance to catch up with some sleep.

Flight Attendant

Hotel Manager

What is a hotel manager?

Hotel managers make sure that the hotels they are responsible for run properly, are safe places to stay, have good staff and make a profit.

Some hotels have thousands of guests staying at the same time.

Hotels provide accommodation for guests, and they are also used for:
- business affairs, such as meetings, **seminars** and conferences;
- exhibitions, which are often run by societies and hobby groups such as stamp collectors, photographers or artists;
- weddings, parties and celebrations.

Hotels vary in size, ranging from small, family-run businesses with around a dozen bedrooms to huge, **multinational companies** made up of many hotels, often with hundreds of bedrooms.

Managers of small hotels are personally responsible for the smooth running of the entire operation. Managers of large hotels oversee the work of departmental heads working in areas such as catering, housekeeping, marketing and finance.

So you want to work in travel and tourism?

Ice hotels

Ice hotels are a growing tourist attraction in countries within the Arctic Circle. They are made from blocks of ice. New ones are built every year and they are used for around three months until the temperature rises and the ice melts. Many ice hotels are big and have a large number of bedrooms, several restaurants and even cinemas.

Couples often choose to marry in a hotel and hold a party there afterwards.

In large hotels, managers have less direct contact with guests than do managers working in smaller hotels. In large hotels, managers supervise other members of staff and make sure they do their jobs properly.

Hotel managers work long, unsocial hours and are often on duty in the evening and at weekends. They usually live in accommodation at, or near, their hotel.

Main tasks of a hotel manager

Hotel managers make sure that hotels are well-run and are places where guests want to come and stay.

In smaller hotels, managers do a great deal of the work themselves. They:
- look after people working in the hotel, recruit new staff, and train staff;
- supervise employees, giving instructions and making sure that people are working well together;
- control stock by checking and ordering supplies such as cleaning materials, linen (sheets, towels and pillowcases) and crockery when needed;
- make sure the hotel building is in good condition and organize repairs and redecoration inside and outside when necessary;
- deal with customers, making sure they are comfortable, and sort out any complaints;
- control finances by keeping accounts and planning budgets.

Keeping staff informed of any changes is part of the job of the hotel manager.

Good points and bad points

'Hotel management is in my blood. I started off working as a night porter while at school and enjoyed hotel life so much I made it my career.'

'You have to love the work to do it, because the hours can be very long. When you first begin, you often work seven days in a row.'

Managers working in large hotels lead a team of departmental heads including:
- the restaurant manager, who is in charge of planning menus, buying ingredients and overseeing food preparation;
- the domestic services manager, who is responsible for making sure the bedrooms and public rooms are clean and tidy and that the linen is washed and ready for use when needed. This manager checks the guest diary for details of arrivals and departures and makes sure that rooms are ready for guests;
- the personnel manager, whose job includes recruiting, training and supervising staff.

Hotel managers hold regular meetings with department managers to talk over problems and check that all is well. If a hotel is part of a large group or chain, decisions are often made at headquarters and passed on to hotel managers, who carry out the tasks.

If guests enjoy their stay they will come back again and recommend the hotel to other people.

Hotel Manager 23

Skills needed to be a hotel manager

Organizational abilities
Hotel managers need to organize the work of others, and to do this they must be organized themselves.

Leadership
Managers in all areas of work need to encourage people to do well. People work much more efficiently if they are happy and feel appreciated.

Communication skills
Hotel managers need to give instructions to other people and to write letters and reports, so they must speak and write in a way that is clear and easily understood.

Presence of mind
In a busy hotel there is sure to be the occasional crisis. If anything goes wrong, such as rooms being over-booked or a guest becoming ill, the hotel manager must act quickly and confidently to sort out the problem.

Numeracy
Hotel managers are in charge of the accounts – these are the financial records that show how much a hotel is costing to run and the amount of money it is making. The managers have to make sure that the accounts are kept up-to-date and in order.

Adaptability
Managers must be able to take over different jobs in a crisis, for example, when a member of staff is ill or everyone else is busy.

In a hotel, problems need to be solved quickly.

Hotel managers keep in close contact with all areas of work.

Language skills
The ability to speak a foreign language is not essential but it is useful. As more people travel abroad on business and on holiday, there is a growing demand for hotel managers who speak at least one foreign language. This also means that hotel managers with language skills can work abroad if they wish.

fact file

Hotel managers may start out by taking a degree or a diploma in hotel management. Qualifications are important, but employers are also looking for outgoing, lively, sociable people who have a real interest in the work. It is useful to know what the job involves from work experience, or holiday or part time work in bars, restaurants and hotels.

A day in the life of a hotel manager

Anna Holden

Anna Holden works as a manager in a large hotel.

9.00 am — I meet with department managers to update them on sales figures. This meeting deals with the number of bookings and major expenses. Afterwards, department managers report to me on what is happening in their areas.

10.00 am — I settle down to writing letters and reports, sending emails and making phone calls.

11.30 am — Time for my daily tour of the hotel. This is when I see for myself exactly what is going on and speak to as many staff as possible. The only way to run a hotel efficiently is to keep in touch with what is happening in each area.

1.00 pm — I meet the marketing manager for lunch. Today he is also meeting with the director of a large company who might hold conferences in the hotel. I have lunch with them both and do my best to encourage the company director to use the hotel.

2.30 pm — I lead a meeting about the possible redecoration of the hotel. This promises to be a big job and will involve the hotel being closed for several weeks, so there is a lot to be considered.

4.00 pm — I go through a pile of guest comment cards. All guests are asked to fill in a card, saying how they found the accommodation, service and food at the hotel. This gives us valuable information about ways in which the hotel could be improved.

6.30 pm I attend a meeting to discuss ways of bringing more tourists into the area. Local restaurant owners, shop managers and tourist officers are there because the more people we bring in, the more all our businesses will flourish.

A final check of the restaurant to make sure that everything is in order.

A hotel manager must oversee the ordering and delivery of supplies.

Hotel Manager 27

Theme Park Attractions Manager

What is a theme park attractions manager?

Theme park attractions managers control the operation of the many theme parks that are springing up all over the world and attracting millions of visitors every year. As their name suggests, theme parks tend to be constructed around a particular idea, or theme. The many different themes include parks devoted to wild animals, cartoon characters, fairy tales and space travel. There are also water parks where visitors spend their time swimming in different pools, taking water rides and shooting down **flumes**.

Water parks are very popular, especially on hot days.

One reason that theme parks are so popular is that they have something to offer the whole family, from toddlers to grandparents. The attractions range from exciting, even terrifying rides to children's rides and family restaurants.

The job of a theme park manager may involve being in overall charge of the park, or he or she may control just one area of the operation.

The world according to Disney

In 1955 a theme park called Disneyland opened in Anaheim, California, USA. It occupied 160 acres of land. This was followed by Disneyworld in Florida, which opened in 1971. In 1992 Disney came to Europe with the opening of Disneyland Paris in France.

Today, Walt Disney World in Florida is made up of Epcot, the Magic Kingdom Park, the Downtown Disney Area, the Disney-MGM Studios and Disney's Animal Kingdom Park. It represents almost half of the tourism industry in the state of Florida.

Either way, the job includes:

- finance – keeping a check on what it costs to run the park, and balancing this against the money made from customers;
- marketing – thinking of ways in which the park can be made even more successful and making sure that people who are likely to enjoy it hear about it and come and visit;
- promotions – organizing special events, such as carnivals, parades, competitions and parties to encourage people to visit the park.

Behind the fun, a theme park has to be a very well-organized operation. It employs hundreds, if not thousands, of people. The task of making sure that other people have fun is not as easy as it seems.

Successful theme parks have been developed in countries all over the world.

Theme Park Attractions Manager

Main tasks of a theme park attractions manager

General theme park managers are responsible for every area. It is their job to make sure the park is well-run, safe and popular. The managers of the different departments work under the supervision of the general manager. The departments include:

Technical and maintenance
Theme parks always need new, exciting rides and attractions. The manager in charge of this department looks after the **installation** of new equipment and the maintenance work, which ensures everything is working well. This behind-the-scenes work goes on all the time. The manager is also in charge of safety. While the theme park rides may appear to be dangerous, they must be completely safe.

Rides and attractions are checked regularly to make sure they are safe.

Good points and bad points

'The atmosphere in the park is great. Families are here to enjoy themselves and the staff are lively and enthusiastic.''

'But it is important to remember that making sure other people have fun is not the same as having fun yourself. Dressing up as a cuddly animal in a heatwave is not at all comfortable!'

So you want to work in travel and tourism?

Finance
The manager in charge of finance keeps accounts of the costs and income of the park and prepares reports to show how much money is made and spent by each department.

Planning and development
The manager in charge of planning and development oversees the design of new attractions, rides, shows, hotels and restaurants. He or she also searches for new locations and thinks of ideas for future theme parks.

Marketing
The marketing manager looks at ways of encouraging visitors to the theme park through advertising in magazines and newspapers, running competitions with free trips as prizes, and **sponsoring** sports events which draw attention to the theme park's existence.

Personnel
The manager in charge of this department must find the right people to work in the park and make sure they receive appropriate training. The manager needs to employ staff in the following areas:
- technical – working on repairs and maintenance;
- administrative – taking bookings, making phone calls, writing reports and letters;
- cleaning and catering – keeping the park tidy and visitors well-fed;
- casting – meeting and greeting the public. Members of staff in this area are often dressed in costumes, for example as cartoon characters.

Meeting favourite cartoon characters is a dream come true.

Skills needed by a theme park attractions manager

Theme park attractions managers must:

- get on well with people of all types;
- have good leadership skills – be fair but firm, and able to make decisions and convince other people to accept them;
- have good communication skills to be able to write and speak in a clear, direct way.

Managers working in particular areas need special skills, as shown below.

Technical expertise
Technical managers must understand the technology behind the attractions and know exactly how each ride works. They need to have an eye for detail so that they notice the smallest change in the way a ride is operating.

Health and safety
Technical managers must also be experienced health and safety officers. They must make sure that the park is a safe place in which visitors can relax and enjoy themselves.

Numeracy
Financial managers need to be very good with figures. They are usually qualified accountants.

Enjoying yourself is hungry work.

Work in a theme park goes on well into the evening.

Marketing
Marketing and promotional managers need good imaginations, because their ideas make the theme park attractive to the public. They also need to know a great deal about the entertainment industry, to understand the latest trends, and make sure the park offers the most up-to-date attractions to visitors.

Personnel
Personnel managers should be tactful and able to deal with difficult situations. They need a good knowledge of employment law.

fact file

Some theme parks offer management trainee posts for people who wish to gain experience of working there. Most people, however, start working as theme park attractions managers after having gained qualifications and experience of work in other areas, for example in leisure centres or hotel management.

A day with a theme park attractions manager

Simon Gill

Simon Gill is a technical manager at a water park.

8.30 am   Even at this early hour, the park is full of visitors. Much of our work is behind the scenes, such as ensuring machinery is operating properly, and running safety checks. If there is a serious problem an attraction may need to be closed, but we do our best to avoid this happening. I brief my team and make sure that everyone knows what they are doing.

9.30 am   I go on an inspection of park attractions. My mobile phone is switched on so that I can be contacted immediately if I'm needed.

12.00 pm   Everything seems to be going well. I'm back in my office checking reports. We have to keep records of all the work carried out on attractions in all areas of the park.

1.30 pm   I have a quick lunch. It's a hot day and I envy the visitors splashing around in the water. The park is not open all the year round, so my job varies from month to month. During the winter the park is closed for several months because the weather isn't warm enough for people to swim in the open air. This gives us a period during which new attractions can be installed and the whole park can be redecorated and thoroughly **overhauled** ready for the coming season.

2.30 pm   I interview the people who have applied for a job in the maintenance team. Keeping a water park safe and in working order takes a large number of people. All the team members must be well qualified and keen.

5.00 pm   The last interview has finished. The personnel manager was also present at the interviews. She and I discuss which candidate should get the job.

Theme parks are enjoyed by visitors of all ages.

Daily technical checks take place to make sure everything is in order.

Theme Park Attractions Manager   35

Tour Guide

What is a tour guide?

Tour guides are employed by travel companies to make sure that customers who buy holidays from these companies are satisfied with them. Tour guides help customers become acquainted with the holiday area and provide them with a chance to visit places of interest. They look after the holidaymakers and deal with any problems they might have while they are away.

Tour guides may be based at one particular holiday resort throughout the season, or they may travel with a group of holiday-makers from place to place by coach, plane or cruise ship.

During the holiday season, tour guides are available twenty-four hours a day to deal with emergencies, such as sudden illness, or holidaymakers running

The tour guide's first task is to make sure that everyone has arrived safely.

36 So you want to work in travel and tourism?

> ### The importance of tourism
> The tourist industry is the world's largest employer. In Europe and North America, holidays and travel for enjoyment are the third largest household expense for families, after food and heating.

into trouble, losing their baggage, or being arrested by the local police. Tour guides need to know their holiday area very well so that they can advise visitors on all types of matters, from the best restaurants and nightclubs to local beauty spots.

Tour guides are expected to get to know the holidaymakers in their care and to spend time with them. They work long hours, often late into the night. Their work is usually seasonal, lasting for around six months of the year. Very few tour guides are employed by travel companies all year round.

The outward journey is almost over and the holiday hotel will soon be in sight.

Tour Guide

Main tasks of a tour guide

Tour guides who are based in a particular resort perform a wide range of tasks. These include:
- meeting people when they arrive and dealing with problems such as lost luggage;
- taking the holidaymakers to their accommodation and helping them check in;
- organizing welcome parties and other social events, so holidaymakers get to know each other;
- looking after holidaymakers who are injured or become ill;
- dealing with cases ranging from jellyfish stings and sunburn to sudden heart attacks and broken legs.

Tour guides must deal with holidaymakers' complaints. If the customer complains, for example, about dirty rooms or poor quality food, the tour guide must make sure the complaint is **valid**.

For some holidaymakers, the fun begins when the sun goes down.

Good points and bad points

'I don't have to worry about where I'm sleeping or what I'm eating – that's all looked after for me.'

'I like the challenge of dealing with the unexpected, although matters can get out of hand when serious accidents or illness happen. Then it's very hard supporting relatives, dealing with hospital staff and making arrangements for people to travel home.'

So you want to work in travel and tourism?

If it is, he or she must ensure that things are put right. Guides may also have to deal with complaints about holidaymakers in their care. If, for example, the holidaymakers return to the hotel late at night, make a noise and wake other guests, then the tour guide must tactfully tell them to stop behaving in this way.

Tour guides offer trips and excursions to holidaymakers as part of the **package**. These may include camel or horse rides, boat trips, and visits to cities, beauty spots and nightclubs. Finally the tour guides must make sure that holidaymakers leave with their passports and luggage at the end of their stay.

Tour guides who travel from place to place with groups of tourists have additional responsibilities. These include:
- accompanying tourists on trips;
- providing information or commentaries;
- dealing with travel arrangements during the holiday;
- looking after tickets for the group.

Guides working on special interest holidays, such as hiking trips or pony treks, need to have specialist knowledge. These holidays give people an opportunity to learn more about a particular subject. For example, when visiting an area, they learn about its natural life or history.

Tour guides need to know a great deal about the places they visit.

Tour Guide 39

Skills needed to be a tour guide

Enthusiasm
Tour guides should enjoy their job and encourage holidaymakers to have a good time. This means they must be positive, lively and friendly, even when they feel tired and in need of a rest.

Tact
It is not easy dealing with people's complaints. Sometimes tour guides have to explain to customers that they cannot have what they want. For example, a family might be disappointed with their accommodation. If the resort is full, however, the tour guide may not be able to move them to the accommodation of their choosing. The tour guide needs to be able to handle this difficult situation tactfully and firmly.

Tour guides help tourists to get to know their holiday area.

Confidence
Holidaymakers need to feel safe and well looked after. When difficulties arise, such as travel delays or over-bookings in a hotel, the customers expect the tour guide to put matters right as quickly as possible. Guides should appear capable of coping with any situation, even when they are not sure what to do.

Physical fitness and stamina
The work is hard and the hours are long. Guides who take tourists out to clubs until late at night will still need to be up early the next day, giving advice on where to shop and which beaches to visit.

So you want to work in travel and tourism?

A tour guide is responsible for the safety of all the passengers on their tour.

Self reliance

Tour guides must be happy with their own company. While they spend a lot of time being friendly to large groups of people, tour guides have to cope with a working life spent apart from close friends or family. They work away from home, looking after the needs of successive groups of holidaymakers, so they do not often get the opportunity to make close relationships.

fact file

Tour guides may have studied for a degree in travel and tourism. People often work as tour guides for a short time before settling down to follow other careers. Working as a tour guide brings with it a chance to travel and see the world and, in some cases, to follow a particular interest such as skiing, sailing or walking.

A day in the life of a tour guide

Mary Rosen

Mary Rosen is a tour guide in a lively Spanish seaside resort.

4.00 am My alarm goes off and I get up and get dressed. I then board the coach taking tourists who have just finished their holiday from the resort to the airport.

5.30 am Although one family is late boarding the coach, we make up the time and arrive at the airport promptly.

7.00 am I wave the group off home and pick up the new arrivals. One person's luggage is lost. I will have to phone the airport later today to see if it's been traced.

8.30 am All the customers are settling into their hotel or apartment. They are coming to a welcome barbecue and disco tonight. Everyone is happy – so far!

9.30 am I chat with the hotel manager. Guests have complained about the lack of hot water and I ask him to look into this problem.

11.00 am The lost luggage has been found. I drive out to the airport and pick it up.

1.30 pm I rest for a couple of hours so that I am ready for tonight.

4.00 pm A call from a mother about her daughter. She is three years old, has been out in the sun for six hours and is hot and feverish. I call the local **pharmacy** and am instructed to keep the child

42 So you want to work in travel and tourism?

cool and quiet and give her plenty of liquids. If she is still unwell after a few hours she will need to see a doctor.

6.30 pm I check the arrangements for the barbecue and put out all my leaflets and information. I phone about the sick child. Her temperature has returned to normal and she is asleep.

8.00 pm My talk begins. I describe possible trips, recommend clubs and restaurants and answer questions from holidaymakers.

12.15 am The barbecue is in full swing and everyone is enjoying themselves.

A tour guide can help everyone to relax and enjoy their holiday.

One group leaves and very soon another will arrive.

Tour Guide 43

Travel Agent

What is a travel agent?

Travel agents sell holidays and make travel arrangements for business customers. Holidays used to be a seasonal occurrence: people would book their holidays six months in advance and take them during the summer. Now holidays are an all year round activity. Many families go away for Christmas and Easter, and weekend breaks have become very popular.

Every year, large numbers of people travel for pleasure.

There are two types of travel agent, dealing with leisure and business travel. Leisure travel agents usually have their offices in shopping centres, so that shoppers can drop in easily to discuss their holiday plans. Clients can buy a holiday that includes travel and accommodation to a particular resort, or a cruise that is paid for in advance. These types of holidays are called **package tours**. Leisure travel agents also organize individual holidays for clients who want the freedom to travel where they like, and who do not want to spend their holiday touring with the same group of people.

44 So you want to work in travel and tourism?

The power of the Internet

Travel agents have been facing increasing competition from bookings being made on the Internet. It is now commonplace for people to arrange their own holidays (packages, flights and insurance) on their home computers, without having to consult a travel agent. However, there is still some demand for travel agents, with many people preferring the one-to-one contact with a professional when organizing their holidays.

Business travel agents are an important part of the travel industry. They make all the travel arrangements for a particular company or organization.

Business clients are vital to the success of the travel industry.

Travel agents use computers to check whether holidays and flights are available and make bookings for customers. An increasing number of people are using the Internet or the telephone to book holidays and make travel arrangements.

Main tasks of a travel agent

Leisure travel agents talk to clients about:
- what they want from a holiday, the country or area they want to visit and their budget (the amount of money they have to spend);
- the type of resort they are looking for, such as a quiet place where they can relax, or a lively resort with lots of entertainment.

The agent helps the clients choose:
- their accommodation, be it a large luxury hotel, a small locally run hotel or a self-catering apartment;
- the options for leisure activities, such as sailing, walking, swimming, sunbathing, or sightseeing.

Once the travel agents have a good idea of what a customer wants, they can recommend resorts and locations.

It is important to find the right holiday to suit the clients' needs.

Good points and bad points

'I like getting to know people and finding out what type of holiday they are looking for. It pays to put some thought into what you want from a holiday, because it will be costing you a lot of money.'

'When things go wrong, people are very disappointed. That's why I'm always worried when people rush in and say they want to go away in a week's time and don't care where they go.'

46 So you want to work in travel and tourism?

Most holiday bookings are done by computer.

When customers have decided where they want to go, the travel agents:
- make the bookings and supply tickets;
- arrange holiday insurance and **travellers' cheques** and advise on **vaccinations**, **visas** and passports.

Business travel agents are not found in the high street. Their names are not well known, but they deal with a huge amount of business. These travel agencies, or travel management companies, compete with one another to take on the travel arrangements of large organizations for a set period, perhaps one or two years.

The travel agency's job is to:
- make sure that the organization's employees who travel for business have trouble-free journeys;
- ensure that the organization gets the cheapest prices;
- fit travel plans around business schedules, booking suitable flights, and organizing accommodation;
- arrange conference facilities, where necessary, and book rail tickets and car hire.

Travel Agent

Skills needed to be a travel agent

Communication
Travel agents must be good communicators – with the ability to write and speak clearly. Customers need to be able to understand what the travel agent is saying, and the letters, reports and messages he or she writes must be easy to follow.

Enthusiasm
An active interest in people and travel is vital. To find the best holiday for their clients, travel agents must encourage people to talk about what they want. They also need to know a great deal about different holiday destinations.

Tact and patience
When something goes wrong, customers can become very disappointed and upset. Travel agents have to deal with these situations and discuss the problem calmly with the customer.

Flexibility
Travel agents often need to solve problems and come up with alternative ideas. For example, if there is not a convenient connection between two flights, the agents need to suggest alternative flights, overnight hotel stops, car hire or train or bus travel.

Some travel agents specialise in winter sports holidays.

48 So you want to work in travel and tourism?

Travel agents help customers plan their trips down to the finest detail.

fact file

Many travel agents have a degree or diploma in travel or tourism. People wanting to work in the travel industry usually start at the bottom and learn on the job, whatever their qualifications.

IT skills

Computers are used widely in the travel industry, so travel agents must understand how to operate them to find the information they need.

Eye for detail

If the travel agent overlooks a small detail it can ruin a client's holiday. Foreign visitors need a **visa** to visit some countries. It is the travel agent's job to remind customers of this and organize a visa for them. Bookings can become very complicated especially when they involve different **time zones**.

Travel Agent

A day in the life of a travel agent

Theresa James

Theresa James is the manager of a leisure travel agency.

8.30 am — I carry out a security check at the office. This involves switching off the burglar alarm and switching on the computers. Then there's a staff briefing about the day ahead.

9.00 am — Business is slow at first, so we tidy the shop and I make some phone calls and open the post.

10.30 am — A couple wanting to get married abroad come into the office. I discuss possible holiday destinations with them and give them some brochures. They are keen to marry soon and want to invite about twenty-five guests. Some of the guests want to stay in the resort after the wedding, while others want to move on elsewhere. The couple ask a lot of questions. Can they marry on a beach? Will the ceremony be in English? How will the wedding dress be transported?

12.00 pm — One of the computer stations is not working properly. I phone the helpline and an adviser talks me through the problem. After this the computer works fine, but – as is usually the case with these problems – it takes a while to get up and running again.

Travel agents can help couples organize a dream wedding in a romantic location.

50 So you want to work in travel and tourism?

1.00 pm I take a break for a sandwich.

1.25 pm My wedding couple return. They have decided to marry in the Caribbean. I give them some idea of prices and different grades of accommodation. They're not sure now about the number of guests, but promise to let me know within a week. We need to come to a decision soon to guarantee that this number of people can have the holiday they want.

4.00 pm The shop is quieter now, so I chat with the team about their day. I catch up with a few phone calls and some paperwork.

6.00 pm I've shut down the computers, checked that the burglar alarm is switched on, locked up and I'm on my way home. Sometimes I feel I could do with a good holiday myself!

As a travel agent it is rewarding to learn that people have enjoyed their holiday.

Travel Agent 51

Travel Writer

What is a travel writer?

There are many different types of travel writer. Some are journalists employed by a newspaper or magazine and paid a salary to write regular travel articles. Others are **freelance** authors who sell articles to publications. Their income helps to pay for their own travels.

Some travel writers work on guidebooks, which give a great deal of information about a particular area. Others are involved in writing brochures. These are leaflets providing information about a place, usually with lots of brightly coloured photographs. Travel companies often use freelance writers to do this work.

Sometimes travel writers are involved in personal projects, which may take the form of a personal account of an individual living or travelling in a foreign country. These books or articles are usually full of amusing descriptions to give the reader a good idea of life abroad.

Reading travel guides can give tourists a lot of useful information about particular areas of interest.

Continental drift

Bill Bryson's amusing and thoughtful books about life in different countries have made him famous. Bryson gave up college in the USA and settled in the UK, where he became a journalist. His travel writing began when he took a car trip around the USA to relive holidays he had experienced as a child. He wrote a book called *The Lost Continent* about his journey. Bryson does not call himself a travel writer, but a 'tourist who writes books'.

Writers may be commissioned to do the work. This means that a publisher formally agrees to buy the book when it is written. Otherwise the writers may finish the book first, and then try to sell it to a publisher. All travel writers have their own individual ways of working. For some people it is a full-time job; for others it is an interesting hobby.

Guides often include maps and sometimes bus and train times.

Main tasks of a travel writer

Travel writing sounds like a dream job – imagine researching and writing for part of the time, then making enough money to travel the world and have adventures the rest of the time. The reality, however, is less glamorous and the life suits only a few people. Most travel writers live on a small budget with no idea of what their next job will be. Long periods of travel can be tiring and uncomfortable.

Journalists who work on travel magazines
These writers may do some travelling themselves, but often they are based in offices. Their work includes:
- researching material for articles, suggesting new places to cover, and writing;
- commissioning articles, which means finding authors to write articles and deciding how much to pay them;
- sometimes being involved in organizing photography, finding illustrations and designing travel pages.

Travel writers often take photographs for their books.

Good points and bad points

'I love visiting different countries and passing on what I have seen to other people.'

'The work can be exhausting and frustrating, especially when I'm behind with my writing deadlines. Planes are delayed, buses don't appear and trains are cancelled.'

54 So you want to work in travel and tourism?

Travel guides help tourists make the most of their holidays.

Travel writers working on guidebooks

Guidebooks include information on where to stay and to eat, local places of interest, buses and trains, history and customs. Their writers need to gather a lot of detailed information. They often live in the area covered by the guidebook, so they are very well informed.

Travel writers who produce brochures

Writers working on brochures usually use material supplied to them and so are not likely to travel much.

People who write about their personal experiences while travelling tend to have other jobs and, for some of them, writing is a hobby. Very few people make a fortune at travel writing, but they still enjoy it. One example of success, however, is Peter Mayle, who retired from his job in advertising to live in France. He wrote a book of his experiences called *A Year in Provence*, which became an international bestseller. He followed it with a number of other successful books.

Travel Writer

Skills needed to be a travel writer

Excellent writing skills
Guidebook authors need to write clearly and to pack a great deal of factual information into their writing. Personal travel writers should create a vivid picture of what life is like abroad so that armchair readers feel that they are there with the author.

Mental and physical strength
Travelling can be frustrating, lonely and exhausting. Travel writers must be able to cope with problems as they crop up.

Keyboard skills
Writers need to be able to produce their articles quickly and often in uncomfortable surroundings.

Internet skills
Travel writers need to use the Internet with confidence to find out information about different places and send their material to their editors. Internet cafés, where travellers can use the Internet and write and receive emails, are now found across the world.

Sometimes travel writers work in remote locations.

So you want to work in travel and tourism?

Many people read travel articles in newspapers and magazines to help plan their holidays.

Observation skills
Successful travel writing depends on noticing and writing about the small details that fascinate readers and make them feel they are in the place being described.

Photographic skills
It is useful for travel writers to be familiar with using a camera so that they can provide photographs with their work.

fact file

Journalists writing for a newspaper or magazine usually have a university degree and a further qualification in journalism. The qualifications necessary to become a travel writer, however, are not so clearly defined. People writing occasional travel articles can come from any background. Guidebook writers must have an excellent knowledge of the area they intend to cover, which usually involves staying or living there for some time.

Travel Writer   57

A day in the life of a travel writer

Maria Hardy

Maria Hardy lives in Greece where she teaches English and writes guidebooks.

8.30 am I'm not teaching today so I can do some writing. At the moment I'm updating a travel guide. There's a team of us on the job and I'm covering a number of Greek islands including the one where I live. A guidebook must be updated frequently. For example, a couple of years ago a new airport opened at Athens. This meant that the information in all the guidebooks about air travel to and from Athens was out of date.

9.30 am I'm using the Internet for a lot of early research. I can check bus, train and ferry routes and whether hotels and restaurants have changed owners or closed down. Local tourist information offices are also very helpful.

12.30 pm The temperature is beginning to soar and everyone is taking a rest. I doze in a chair and then plan a schedule of visits. Once my initial research is finished, I shall spend all my free time visiting places and making notes.

4.00 pm I get to work on letters and emails sent by my editor. Travellers often contact the guide publishers with their own information – for example, they may have found a new restaurant, or they may have complaints about a bar we've recommended or news that a museum closes on a Monday. This is very helpful, but I still have to check it out before putting it in the guide.

7.45 pm I receive a phone call from another writer who can't get hold of ferry timetables and needs my help.

8.30 pm Time to finish work and meet some friends for a meal in a local **taverna**.

Time to send that article off to the editor.

Travel writers need to make sure information is correct before they include it in a guide.

Glossary

cadets – junior members of the crew who are receiving training.

cancelled – does not run or take place.

cargo – goods transported by ship, for example, coal, machinery or grain.

casino – a place where people can gamble or place bets.

commercial – run to make a profit.

customs and immigration procedures – the checking of passports and papers before people are allowed into a foreign country.

duty-free goods – objects sold more cheaply than usual because taxes are not charged on them.

flumes – water slides.

freelance – working for lots of different companies rather than having a single employer.

glamorous – attractive and exciting.

ingredients – items that are mixed together to make something.

installation – putting a piece of equipment in place, connecting it and making sure it works properly.

international – contact between different countries.

jet lag – tiredness caused by long journeys by air.

legal – lawful.

merchandise – goods such as perfume and alcohol sold during a plane journey.

multinational companies – organizations which have branches in a number of different countries.

navigate/navigating/navigation – to keep on the right course, directing the person in control of a ship, plane or car.

night porter – a member of staff who sits in the reception area of a hotel to deal with late arrivals and any problems that arise during the night.

overhauled – checked to make sure everything is in place and in good condition.

package tours – holidays where people pay a travel company to organize their travel and accommodation for them.

pharmacy – a place where medicines can be bought.

publicity – mention of an event or resort on radio, television or in the newspaper to encourage people to attend.

radar – stands for Radio Direction and Ranging. It is a system for locating objects in space. Using radar, pilots are able to land planes at airports in thick fog.

resorts – towns and villages which attract a large number of holiday makers.

seminars – talks or lectures.

sponsored/sponsoring – giving money for someone to carry out a task. Sponsored students are given money by people or organizations to carry out their studies.

taverna – a Greek inn.

time zone – there are 24 time zones in the world. They are all the same width, and run from the North Pole to the South Pole. When you travel eastwards into a new time zone you move an hour ahead. When you travel west into a new time zone you lose an hour.

travellers' cheques – slips of paper given out by a bank, which people can sign and exchange for money when they are abroad.

updated – checked to make sure the information is correct.

vaccination – an injection into the body which protects a person from catching a certain disease.

valid – legal, not false.

ventilation – way of getting fresh air into a room.

visa – the official papers needed for a person to enter a country.

watch – a shift on board ship when a person is responsible for making sure the ship is moving in the right direction and that there are no problems.

Glossary

Further Information

So do you still want to work in travel and tourism?

There is something very exciting about travel, whether you are on the move yourself, or helping other people to see the world. This book does not aim to cover every job in the travel and tourism industry. What it does hope to do is give you an idea of what working in travel and tourism is like.

Many of the jobs involve working away from home and putting in long hours, including evenings and weekends. This means you have little time for a social life outside work. To work in travel and tourism you need to like people and be prepared to listen to them, even when they are being difficult and demanding.

The way to discover if a job in travel and tourism is right for you, is to find out for yourself what it involves. Read as much as you can on the subject and try to talk to people who work in the industry.

If you are at secondary school and seriously interested in a certain career, ask your careers teacher if he or she could arrange for some work experience. This means spending some time, usually a week or two, in an area of your chosen profession, say a travel agency or hotel, watching what goes on and how the people use their time.

Books

If you want to find out more about working in travel and tourism, you will find the following helpful:

Careers and Jobs in Travel and Tourism, written by Verite Reily Collins, published by Kogan Page, 2004.

Getting into Hotels and Catering, written by Beryl Dixon, published by Trotman, 2002.

Working in Tourism: The UK, Europe and Beyond – For Seasonal and Permanent Staff, written by Verite Reily Collins, published by Vacation – Work, 2004.

Websites

The website addresses (URLs) included in this book were valid at the time of going to press. However, because of the nature of the Internet, it is possible that some addresses may have changed, or sites may have changed or closed down since publication. While the author and Publisher regret any inconvenience this may cause the readers, no responsibility for any such changes can be accepted by either the author or the Publisher.

Useful addresses

General

Prospects, the UK's official graduate careers website
www.prospects.ac.uk

Careers Scotland
www.careers-scotland.org.uk

Connexions Direct
www.connexions-direct.com

Travel and tourism

Association of British Travel Agents Limited (ABTA),
68-71 Newman Street,
London W1T 3AH
Tel: 020 7637 2444
www.abta.com

Guild of Registered Tourist Guides
The Guild House
52D Borough High Street
London
SE1 1XN
Tel: 020 7403 1115
www.blue-badge-guides.com

Guild of Travel Management Companies (GTMC)
Queens House
180-182 Tottenham Court Road London W1T 7PD
Tel: 020 7637 1091
www.gtmc.org

Institute of Travel & Tourism (ITT)
PO Box 217
Ware SG12 8WY
Tel: 0870 770 7960
www.itt.co.uk

People 1st
2nd Floor
Armstrong House
38 Market Square
Uxbridge UB8 1LH
Tel: 0870 060 2550
www.people1st.co.uk

Springboard UK Limited
3 Denmark Street
London WC2H 8L
Tel: 020 7497 8654
www.springboarduk.org.uk

TTC Training (part of Carter & Carter Group plc)
The Quayside
4 Furnival Road
Sheffield S4 7YA
Tel: 0800 915 9396
www.ttctraining.co.uk

Further Information

Index

captain 4, 14
complaints 38, 39, 42
computer 26, 45, 47, 50, 51
crew
  plane 12, 16
  ship 5, 7, 8, 9
cruise liner officer 4-11
  cadet 9
  deck officer 6, 10
  engineering officer 7
  watch system 7
customer service 14, 15, 17, 22

finance 22, 24, 26, 29, 31, 32
first aid 15, 16, 38, 42-43
flight 12, 13, 15, 18, 45, 48
  airport 19
flight attendant 12-19
foreign languages 25

homesickness 8, 41
hotel manager 20-27
  department manager 23

ice hotels 21
internet 45, 56, 58

location 11, 14, 31, 46, 50, 56
luggage 19, 38, 39, 42

marketing 29, 31, 33

package tours 12, 39, 44
passengers
  plane 12, 13, 14, 15, 16, 17
  ship 4, 5, 6, 9, 10
photography 54, 57

qualifications 9, 17, 25, 33, 41, 49, 57

resort 5
  choosing 44, 46, 50
  holiday 36, 38, 39, 40, 42

safety 7, 10, 12, 14, 20, 30, 32, 41
ship 4-11, 36
  cargo 4
  deck 5, 6
  engine 5, 7, 8
  navigation 5, 10
  port 4
sponsorship 9, 31

theme park 28-35
  Disneyland 29
  water park 28
theme park attractions manager 28-35
  administrative work 31
  casting 31
  catering / cleaning 31
  personnel manager 31, 33
  technical manager 31, 32, 34, 35
tickets 39, 47
tour guide 10, 36-43
travel agent 44-51
travel writer 52-59
  Bill Bryson 53
  brochures 53, 55
  guidebooks 52, 55, 56, 58, 59
  magazines 52, 54, 57
  publisher 53, 58